A Kitchen

Classical and Unic

By
Umm Maryam
Copyright © 2015 by Saxonberg Associates
All rights reserved

Published by
BookSumo, a division of Saxonberg Associates
http://www.booksumo.com/

A Gift From Me To You...

I know you like cultural food. But what about Japanese Sushi?

Join my private mailing list of readers and get a copy of *Infinite Sushi: A Complete Set of Sushi and Japanese Recipes* by fellow BookSumo author Hashimoto Kazuma for FREE!

http://booksumo.com/a-kitchen-in-persia-classical-persian-recipes/

Enjoy some of the best sushi available!

You will also receive updates about all my new books when they are free. So please show your support.

Also don't forget to like and subscribe on the social networks. I love meeting my readers. Links to all my profiles are below so please click and connect :)

Facebook

Twitter

Google +

INTRODUCTION

Hello, my friend. I would like to thank you personally for taking the time to purchase my book: *A Kitchen in Persia: Classical and Unique Persian Recipes*. I truly do hope that these recipes are reaching you in the best of health and a period of happiness.

In writing this book I have taken the time to compile, what I believe to be, the simplest and easiest, classical Persian dishes into one source for those of my readers who are cultural food lovers.

After publishing my first book: *Arabia & Asia: A Cookbook with Recipes from Egypt, Morocco, Persia, & Pakistan* I noticed a strong interest in this type of food. So I made the decision to continue this cooking journey by focusing on a new country.

If you are interested in my first cookbook then please see the last few pages of this book where I've provided a link for where to find my seminal cookbook.

If you are interested in any specific type of food then please let me know. I'm very easy to find :)

For each recipe, in *A Kitchen in Persia: Classical and Unique Persian Recipes* you will receive not only ingredients with specific directions. But also accurate information on the amount of time it will take to prepare and cook each dish, so you can plan accordingly before embarking on a specific cooking journey. Each recipe also contains information on its nutritional value as well as serving information. So for health conscience readers check the caloric and fat contents of each dish.

I really want to provide the most value for you, my readers, so I figured this information will help a bit more. I'm constantly trying to improve and I listen to my readers. So please help me with feedback!

You'll find that many of the recipes require rose water. So make sure you check locally or just purchase a few bottles online.

So without further ado, I will stop talking. Let's get our frying pans and food processors ready and take a trip to Persia with some classical dishes!

Table of Contents

Introduction 4
Table of Contents 6
NOTICE TO PRINT READERS: 9
Legal Notes 10
Chapter 1: Classical and Unique Persian Recipes 11
    Ash-e-jow 11
    (Barley Soup) 11
    Khoresh Fesenjan 14
    (Chicken Pomegranate Stew) 14
    Maast-o Khiar 16
    (Cucumber Yogurt) 16
    Kebabs Persian Style 18
    Lubia Polo 20
    (Green Bean Rice) 20
    Kebabs Persian Style II 23
    Fesenjun 25
    Sabzi Polo 27
    (Herb Rice with Fava Beans) 27
    Yogurt Salad Persian Style 30

Walnut Cookies in Persia	32
Herbed Pomegranate Salsa	35
Yazdi Cakes	37
Iskender Kebab	40
Ginger Sekanjabin	43
(Persian Syrup Drink)	43
Tomato Avocado Salad	44
Fereni	46
(Persian Pudding)	46
Sekanjabin	48
(Mint, Ginger, Strawberry Syrup)	48
Adas Polow	50
(Rice and Lentils)	50
Lamb and Asparagus Stew	55
Persian Yogurt Dessert	57
Jarjeer	59
(Arugula Salad)	59
Persian Melon Salad	61
A Gift From Me To You...	63
Come On...	65
Let's Be Friends :)	65
About The Publisher.	66
Can I Ask A Favour?	67

Interested in My Other Cookbooks? 68

NOTICE TO PRINT READERS:

Hey, because you purchased the print version of this book you are entitled to its original digital version for free by Amazon.

So when you have the time, please review your purchases, and download the Kindle version of this book.

You might enjoy consuming this book more in its original digital format.

;)

But, in any case, take care and enjoy reading in whatever format you choose!

LEGAL NOTES

ALL RIGHTS RESERVED. NO PART OF THIS BOOK MAY BE REPRODUCED OR TRANSMITTED IN ANY FORM OR BY ANY MEANS. PHOTOCOPYING, POSTING ONLINE, AND / OR DIGITAL COPYING IS STRICTLY PROHIBITED UNLESS WRITTEN PERMISSION IS GRANTED BY THE BOOK'S PUBLISHING COMPANY. LIMITED USE OF THE BOOK'S TEXT IS PERMITTED FOR USE IN REVIEWS WRITTEN FOR THE PUBLIC AND/OR PUBLIC DOMAIN.

Chapter 1: Classical and Unique Persian Recipes

Ash-e-Jow

(Barley Soup)

Ingredients:

1. 2 quarts chicken stock
2. 2 tbsps vegetable oil
3. one medium onion, diced
4. one cup uncooked pearl barley
5. one tsp turmeric
6. one lime, juiced
7. 1/4 cup tomato paste
8. salt, according to your preference
9. ground black pepper, according to your preference
10. one cup diced carrots
11. 1/2 cup sour cream
12. 1/2 cup chopped fresh parsley
13. 8 lime wedges

Directions:

1. Grab a cooking pot that can be covered. Begin to warm up your chicken stock until it reaches a point of simmering.

2. Grab another pot, add some veggie oil, and get it hot. Once the oil is hot, add some onions and begin to fry them down until they are see-through.
3. Once your onions are translucent combine some pearl barley and stir everything for about one min.
4. After one min of stirring combine the following ingredients taking care to stir: pepper, heated chicken stock, salt, turmeric, tomato paste, and juiced lime.
5. Continue to stir and heat the combined contents until it reaches a boiling point. Once boiling turn the heat down to its lowest setting, and let everything simmer nicely for one hour.
6. After one hour combine your carrots with the mixture and let everything continue to cook for thirty mins. After thirty mins you should notice the carrots are no longer hard and the barley is soft.
7. Now grab a container for mixing, preferably a bowl, and add some sour cream to it.
8. Take one half of a cup of soup, and combine it with the sour cream taking care to mix everything consistently.
9. Slowly combine the sour cream and soup mix with the larger pot of soup, taking care to stir constantly.
10. After adding your sour cream to the soup combine some fresh parsley.
11. The soup is now ready for serving with lime.
12. Enjoy.

NOTE: If you notice that your soup gets too hard or thick, then to fix this, you only have to mix in some extra water.

Serving Size: 8 servings

Preparation	Cooking	Total Time
10 mins	2 hrs	2 hrs 10 mins

Nutritional Information:

Calories	193 kcal
Carbohydrates	28.3 g
Cholesterol	9 mg
Fat	.2 g
Fiber	4.3 g
Protein	5.5 g
Sodium	178 mg

* Percent Daily Values are based on a 2,000 calorie diet.

Khoresh Fesenjan

(Chicken Pomegranate Stew)

Ingredients:

1. 2 tbsps olive oil
2. one 1/2 lbs chicken legs, cut up
3. one white onion, thinly sliced
4. 1/2 lb walnuts, toasted and finely ground in a food processor
5. one tsp salt
6. 4 cups pomegranate juice
7. 1/2 tsp cardamom (optional)
8. 2 tbsps sugar (optional)

Directions:

1. Grab a large pot good for frying, preferably a skillet, and add some olive oil. Get this olive oil nice and hot with a medium level of heat.
2. Once the oil is hot you want to combine, with the oil, your onions, and chicken.
3. Allow everything to fry for about twenty mins. Take care to stir the onions and chicken every once and a while.
4. Now take the following ingredients and combine them with the chicken and onions: cardamom, walnut puree, pomegranate juice, and salt.
5. Continue heating everything until it reaches a boiling point. Once the mixture is boiling, lower the heating source to its lowest level,

place a lid on the pot, and let everything simmer for one and a half hours. Take care to stir the mixture sometimes while it simmers.
6. After simmering for the recommended time (1.5 hours) add some sugar and possibly more seasonings according to your tastes.
7. Allow everything to continue cooking for another 30 mins.
8. Serve and enjoy.

NOTE: If the contents become too thick then make sure you add some additional warm water.

Serving Size: 6 servings

Preparation	Cooking	Total Time
15 mins	2 hrs 30 mins	2 hrs 45 mins

Nutritional Information:

Calories	785 kcal
Carbohydrates	95.4 g
Cholesterol	64 mg
Fat	39 g
Fiber	2.9 g
Protein	24.4 g
Sodium	445 mg

* Percent Daily Values are based on a 2,000 calorie diet.

Maast-o Khiar

(Cucumber Yogurt)

Ingredients:

1. one (32 oz) container plain yogurt
2. 3 cucumbers, peels removed and diced
3. one clove garlic, minced
4. one shallot, finely chopped
5. 5 tbsps dried dill weed
6. one tsp salt
7. one tsp pepper

Directions:

1. Grab a medium sized container good for mixing, preferably a bowl, and combine the following ingredients inside of it: shallot, yogurt, garlic, and cucumbers.
2. Combine the following seasonings with your yogurt mixture: pepper, dill, and salt.
3. After combining all the ingredients place the mixture in the frig for about one hour to allow the mixture to rest and increase in tastiness.
4. Plate and enjoy.

Serving Size: 16 servings

Preparation	Cooking	Total Time
15 mins	1 hr	1 hr 15 mins

Nutritional Information:

Calories	46 kcal
Carbohydrates	6.3 g
Cholesterol	3 mg
Fat	0.9 g
Fiber	0.7 g
Protein	3.8 g
Sodium	188 mg

* Percent Daily Values are based on a 2,000 calorie diet.

Kebabs Persian Style

Ingredients:

1. one (8 oz) container plain low-fat yogurt
2. one onion, chopped
3. 1/2 tsp dried mint
4. 2 lbs beef top sirloin, cut into large cubes

Directions:

1. Grab a large container good for mixing, preferably a bowl.
2. Combine in your container the following ingredients: mint, yogurt, and onion.
3. Combine your beef cubes with the yogurt as well.
4. Cover the contents and place them in the frig for about six hours to marinate.
5. Now we need a hot grill to continue this recipe. The grill should be very hot with a high level of heat.
6. Once your grill is hot put the cubed beef pieces on skewers and put them on the grill. Allow them to cook for about 15 mins taking care to turn them every few mins.
7. Plate and enjoy.

Serving Size: 6 servings

Preparation	Cooking	Total Time
15 mins	15 mins	6 hrs 30 mins

Nutritional Information:

Calories	263 kcal
Carbohydrates	4.4 g
Cholesterol	83 mg
Fat	14.4 g
Fiber	0.3 g
Protein	27.1 g
Sodium	84 mg

* Percent Daily Values are based on a 2,000 calorie diet.

Lubia Polo

(Green Bean Rice)

Ingredients:

1. one lb ground beef
2. one large onion, chopped
3. one jalapeno pepper, finely chopped
4. 2 tbsps curry powder
5. 5 cups chicken broth
6. one cup tomato sauce
7. one lb fresh green beans, cut into one inch pieces
8. 3 cups uncooked basmati rice, rinsed and drained
9. 3 tbsps oil

Directions:

1. Let's begin this recipe with a large cooking pot preferably one that is non-stick. Put the pot over a high level of heat.
2. Once your pot is hot, add your beef to it and cook it down until it has no pinkness. Once your beef has achieved this state combine jalapenos and onions, and allow everything to continue cooking until soft and tender.
3. Combine some curry with the beef and onions for extra seasoning.
4. Mix in your tomato sauce and broth and allow everything to continue cooking until it reaches a boiling state. Once everything is hot and

boiling you want to add your green beans and continue to cook everything for about 15 mins. After 15 mins you should notice that the green beans are tender.

5. Combine your rice with the contents in the pot and place a lid on everything.
6. Turn your heating source lower to about a medium-to-low level and let everything cook for about 20 mins.
7. At this point (after 20 mins) you should notice that a majority of the pot's liquid has evaporated (make sure you do not overcook your rice and make it too soft).
8. Remove everything in the pot into a new dish for storage. Now that the pot is empty add some oil to it and get it hot with a medium level of heating.
9. Now put your rice back into the pot with oil.
10. At this point you want to grab a towel. Be very careful and place the towel or dish towel over the pot.
11. Place a cover on the pot, on top of the towel. Take the end parts of the towel and fold them over the pot's covering.
12. Allow everything to cook for about 35 mins. Take care to not remove the lid on the pot and do not stir anything.
13. After 35 mins take off the cover. Now it's time for some magic.
14. Grab a flat dish or sheet and place it on top of the pot so that it is acting like a lid. Carefully turn the pot upside down and allow the rice to sit on the flat sheet.

15. You should notice the rice keeps the shape of the pot.
16. Enjoy.

Serving Size: 6 servings

Preparation	Cooking	Total Time
20 mins	1 hr 10 mins	1 hr 30 mins

Nutritional Information:

Calories	676 kcal
Carbohydrates	84.8 g
Cholesterol	64 mg
Fat	28.5 g
Fiber	4.9 g
Protein	22.1 g
Sodium	272 mg

* Percent Daily Values are based on a 2,000 calorie diet.

Kebabs Persian Style II

Ingredients:

1. 2 lbs beef tenderloin
2. one onion, chopped
3. one tbsp salt, pepper
4. one juiced lime

Directions:

1. To make this recipe we want to begin by dicing some beef into pieces. Each piece of beef should look like a cube and be about one and one half inches in thickness.
2. Grab a container good for mixing, preferably a bowl, and combine the beef pieces with the following ingredients: lime juice, onion, black pepper, and salt.
3. Combine everything nicely making sure each piece of beef is nicely covered and place the mixture in the frig, covered, for about 8 hours or overnight.
4. Now we need a grill that is nice and hot.
5. Make sure that your grill has a high heating level and place six to eight pieces of skewered beef on the grill for cooking. Take care to oil the grill's surface before putting the beef.
6. Allow the beef pieces to grill for about 4 mins per side. Total time for each piece should be about 16 mins.
7. Plate and enjoy.

Serving Size: 4 servings

Preparation	Cooking	Total Time
20 mins	15 mins	35 mins

Nutritional Information:

Calories	297 kcal
Carbohydrates	3.4 g
Cholesterol	113 mg
Fat	13.5 g
Fiber	0.6 g
Protein	38.4 g
Sodium	1830 mg

* Percent Daily Values are based on a 2,000 calorie diet.

Fesenjun

Ingredients:

1. 2 tbsps olive oil
2. one onion, finely chopped
3. 4 skinless, boneless chicken breast halves
4. one cup finely ground walnuts
5. one (10 fluid oz) bottle pomegranate paste or syrup

Directions:

1. Grab a frying pan preferably a skillet place it over a high level of heating and add some olive oil.
2. Let the oil get hot and then combine some onions with it and fry them until they become soft.
3. Once your onions are soft add your chicken and fry it until you find that all the sides are brown. Once you have browned your chicken and cooked the onions, place the chicken and onions to the side in a separate container.
4. Now you want to add some walnuts to the oil and fry them with a medium level of heat for about ten mins. After 10 mins of frying you should notice that the walnuts have become a bit brown.
5. Take the onions and the chicken that were placed to the side and combine them with the walnuts and mix in your pomegranate paste.

6. Turn the heating source down to its lowest level and place a lid on the pot. Let the contents simmer for about twenty mins. Take care to mix the contents sparingly.
7. Allow everything to cook and simmer until you notice that your chicken is fully cooked. This means that there should be no pinkness in the chicken and also its juices should be clear.
8. Plate and enjoy.

Serving Size: 4 servings

Preparation	Cooking	Total Time
15 mins	30 mins	45 mins

Nutritional Information:

Calories	572 kcal
Carbohydrates	53.2 g
Cholesterol	61 mg
Fat	28.8 g
Fiber	2.5 g
Protein	27.8 g
Sodium	53 mg

* Percent Daily Values are based on a 2,000 calorie diet.

Sabzi Polo

(Herb Rice with Fava Beans)

Ingredients:

1. 6 cups water
2. 4 cups uncooked long-grain white rice
3. 3 tbsps vegetable oil
4. 1/2 cup water
5. one bunch fresh dill, chopped
6. one bunch fresh parsley, chopped
7. one bunch fresh cilantro, chopped
8. 2 cups fresh or frozen fava beans
9. ground turmeric according to your preference
10. ground cinnamon according to your preference
11. one tsp salt
12. one tsp pepper

Directions:

1. To begin this recipe lets grab a pan, possibly a saucepan, something that will be easy for draining. Add some water to this pan and get it to a boiling state.
2. Now grab your rice and continue to run water over it until you notice that the water is running clear.
3. Once you have rinsed the rice properly you want to combine it with the water that is already boiling.
4. You want to allow the rice to continue boiling until you notice it rising to the top of the water.

When you notice this occurring, drain the rice and put it back into the pot.
5. Combine with the waterless rice, some oil and water.
6. Also combine the following ingredients: pepper, dill, salt, parsley, cinnamon, cilantro, turmeric, and fava beans.
7. Allow everything to fry / cook for a bit (about five mins)
8. Lower your heating source to its lowest heating level. Cover the contents and let everything simmer for about 45 mins.
9. Let everything cool. Plate and enjoy.

NOTE: The bottom part of the rice should be crispy like our other recipe, Lubia Polo, make sure to enjoy this very tasty part.

Serving Size: 16 servings

Preparation	Cooking	Total Time
20 mins	55 mins	1 hr 15 mins

Nutritional Information:

Calories	234 kcal
Carbohydrates	44.7 g
Cholesterol	0 mg
Fat	3.1 g
Fiber	2.1 g
Protein	5.5 g
Sodium	214 mg

* Percent Daily Values are based on a 2,000 calorie diet.

YOGURT SALAD PERSIAN STYLE

Ingredients:

1. one (32 oz) container plain yogurt
2. 2 tbsps dried dill weed
3. 2 cloves garlic, minced
4. salt and black pepper according to your preference
5. one cucumber (with seeds and peel removed, and chopped)

Directions:

1. Grab a medium sized container good for mixing, preferably a bowl, and combine the following ingredients in it: pepper, yogurt, salt, dill weed, and garlic.
2. Make sure to combine the contents nicely and then add your cucumber.
3. Place a lid on the container and allow it to rest in the frig for about 8 hours or overnight.
4. Plate and serve.

Serving Size: 8 servings

Preparation	Cooking	Total Time
10 mins		8 hrs 10 mins

Nutritional Information:

Calories	78 kcal
Carbohydrates	9.3 g
Cholesterol	7 mg
Fat	1.8 g
Fiber	0.3 g
Protein	6.3 g
Sodium	154 mg

* Percent Daily Values are based on a 2,000 calorie diet.

Walnut Cookies in Persia

Ingredients:

1. one 1/2 cups finely ground walnuts
2. 3 egg yolks
3. 3/4 cup white sugar
4. one tbsp ground cardamom
5. one tsp baking soda
6. one tbsp rose water
7. one egg yolk
8. one tsp water
9. 1/2 cup walnut pieces for decoration

Directions:

1. To make this recipe we first need to get our ovens nice and hot. So turn the oven on to 350 degrees Fahrenheit, or 175 degrees Celsius.
2. Grab a container of a medium size that is good for mixing, ideally a bowl, and combine the following, taking care to mix everything well: rose water, walnuts grounded, baking soda, three egg yolks, cardamom, and sugar.
3. To continue, we a need a dish safe for baking, possibly a baking sheet.
4. Align the sheet with a layer of parchment or wax paper. We want to place dough on the parchment sheet as tsp sized balls. Take care to provide each cookie with about 2 inches of space from the next cookie.
5. Take your remaining egg yolk and water and mix them.

6. For each cookie you want to take a piece of walnut and push the walnut into the cookie.
7. Once you have added a walnut to your cookie glaze it with the egg yolk and water mixture.
8. At this point your oven should be hot (375 degrees) you want to bake your cookies for twenty mins. After 20 mins the cookies should be a nice brown color.
9. Although the middle of the cookie may seem undone, once you allow the cookies to cool, their hardness will increase.
10. Before removing the cookies from their baking sheet allow them to cool for about ten mins. After ten mins of cooling place the cookies on a rack for extended cooling.
11. Enjoy your dessert.

Serving Size: 36 cookies

Preparation	Cooking	Total Time
15 mins	20 mins	35 mins

Nutritional Information:

Calories	66 kcal
Carbohydrates	5.3 g
Cholesterol	23 mg
Fat	4.8 g
Fiber	0.5 g
Protein	1.3 g
Sodium	36 mg

* Percent Daily Values are based on a 2,000 calorie diet.

Herbed Pomegranate Salsa

Ingredients:

1. one 1/2 sprigs fresh mint, chopped
2. one 1/2 bunches fresh cilantro, chopped
3. one 1/2 bunches Italian flat leaf parsley, chopped
4. one small red onion, chopped
5. one pomegranate, skin and light-colored membrane removed
6. 6 tbsps fresh lime juice
7. 2 tsps grated lime zest
8. one jalapeno pepper, chopped
9. one serrano pepper, chopped
10. one small tomato, diced
11. 2 tbsps olive oil
12. salt according to your preference
13. ground white pepper according to your preference

Directions:

1. Get a container of a medium size and combine the following ingredients in it: olive oil, mint, tomato, cilantro, serrano pepper, italian parsley, jalapeno pepper, red onion, lime zest, pomegranate, and juiced lime.
2. Place a lid over your mixture and put it in the frig for about two hrs.
3. Once everything has chilled-out nicely serve and enjoy.

Serving Size: 4 servings

Preparation	Cooking	Total Time
20 mins		2 hrs 20 mins

Nutritional Information:

Calories	119 kcal
Carbohydrates	14 g
Cholesterol	0 mg
Fat	7.3 g
Fiber	2.5 g
Protein	2.1 g
Sodium	123 mg

* Percent Daily Values are based on a 2,000 calorie diet.

Yazdi Cakes

Ingredients:

1. 2 cups all-purpose flour
2. one tsp baking powder
3. 4 eggs
4. one 1/4 cups white sugar
5. one 1/2 cups butter, melted
6. one cup plain yogurt
7. one 1/2 tsps ground cardamom
8. one tbsp rose water
9. 1/2 cup blanched slivered almonds
10. one 1/2 tbsps chopped pistachio nuts

Directions:

1. So before we begin we want to get our ovens to 375 degrees Fahrenheit or 175 degree Celsius.
2. Grab a sifter and a nice sized bowl and begin to sift your baking powder and flour into this bowl. Once everything has been sifted nicely you want to place everything to the side to rest.
3. Find your baking dish for cupcakes and make sure to coat each section with some non stick cooking spray or veggie oil. You should plan on having about 24 cups of mixture based on this recipe.
4. Get a bowl that you can heat up and mix in the bowl your sugar and eggs. Once you have mixed everything together you want to put this bowl on top of a pan of simmering water.

5. While your pan is over the simmering water you want to mix your eggs with a mixer or whisk for eight mins. After eight mins you should notice the contents have become pale and thicker.
6. Once the contents have reached this thick and pale state you want to take it away from its heating source and keep on whisking for another ten mins.
7. After ten mins of whisking combine the following ingredients: rose water, butter, cardamom, and yogurt. Now you want to combine the flour and also the almonds.
8. Grab a scoop or spoon and put the contents into the cupcake sections. Fill each cupcake section but leave some space for expansion.
9. Before baking, add a covering of pistachios. Enter the cakes into the oven for about 30 mins.

Serving Size: 24 cakes

Preparation	Cooking	Total Time
20 mins	25 mins	45 mins

Nutritional Information:

Calories	215 kcal
Carbohydrates	19.9 g
Cholesterol	62 mg
Fat	14 g
Fiber	0.6 g
Protein	3.4 g
Sodium	121 mg

* Percent Daily Values are based on a 2,000 calorie diet.

Iskender Kebab

Ingredients:

1. 4 pita bread rounds
2. one tbsp olive oil
3. 4 skinless, boneless chicken breast halves - chopped
4. 2 medium onion, chopped
5. one clove garlic, minced
6. one (10.75 oz) can tomato puree
7. ground cumin according to your preference
8. salt according to your preference
9. ground black pepper according to your preference
10. 1/2 cup butter, melted
11. one cup Greek yogurt
12. 1/4 cup chopped fresh parsley

Directions:

1. Before we can begin this recipe we need to get our ovens nice and hot to 350 degrees Fahrenheit or 175 degrees Celsius.
2. Now get a dish that is safe for baking possibly a baking sheet, and place your pita on the sheet. You want to place the pita in the oven and let it get slightly toasted. Once the pita has toasted a bit in the oven, remove it, and slice it into smaller pieces and keep it warm.
3. Grab a frying pan and put some olive oil in it. Heat your olive oil with a medium level of heat. Once the oil is nice and hot you want to mix in

the following ingredients: garlic, chicken, and onion. Fry everything down until your chicken is fully cooked meaning its juices run clear.
4. Now combine with your chicken the following things for seasoning: pepper, tomato puree, salt, and cumin.
5. Allow everything to continue frying for ten additional mins.
6. Get a dish for serving, and place your pita pieces on it. You want to cover the pita pieces with some butter for extra tastiness. Put some of your chicken mixture on top of each pita piece.
7. Put some yogurt on top of the chicken mixture before serving.
8. Enjoy.

Serving Size: 4 servings

Preparation	Cooking	Total Time
15 mins	15 mins	30 mins

Nutritional Information:

Calories	667 kcal
Carbohydrates	48.6 g
Cholesterol	144 mg
Fat	36.2 g
Fiber	3.9 g
Protein	37.3 g
Sodium	886 mg

* Percent Daily Values are based on a 2,000 calorie diet.

Ginger Sekanjabin

(Persian Syrup Drink)

Ingredients:

1. 4 cups white sugar
2. 2 1/2 cups water
3. one cup red or white wine vinegar
4. 1/2 cup minced fresh ginger

Directions:

1. Grab a larger sized pan and get it hot over a high level of heat. Once the pan is hot you want to add some water and sugar and let it begin to boil for about three mins.
2. After three mins take the pan away from its heating source and combine your ginger and vinegar into the mix. Let the contents sit to the side until they have reached the temperature of the room.
3. You now need a sieve. Use your sieve to remove the ginger from the mixture. Continue to let the contents sit at room temperature.
4. When ready to serve use the following formula: 5 parts water to one part of syrup. This mixture should be served frigid.
5. Enjoy.

Tomato Avocado Salad

Ingredients:

1. 4 ripe tomatoes, diced
2. 2 Hass avocados, diced
3. one clove garlic, minced
4. 3 tbsps chopped red onion
5. 6 sprigs cilantro, chopped
6. 2 tbsps fresh lime juice
7. salt and ground black pepper according to your preference
8. one lime, cut into circles

Directions:

1. Get a nice sized container good for mixing.
2. Inside of your container you want to combine the following: cilantro, tomatoes, onion, avocados, and garlic.
3. Once all your contents have been mixed nicely you want to put some juiced lime into the container as well as some pepper and salt.
4. Salad should be served with lime pieces.
5. Enjoy.

Serving Size: 4 servings

Preparation	Cooking	Total Time
20 mins		20 mins

Nutritional Information:

Calories	198 kcal
Carbohydrates	17.3 g
Cholesterol	0 mg
Fat	15.1 g
Fiber	9.2 g
Protein	3.6 g
Sodium	17 mg

* Percent Daily Values are based on a 2,000 calorie diet.

Fereni

(Persian Pudding)

Ingredients:

1. 2/3 cup cornstarch
2. 4 cups milk
3. 6 whole cardamom seeds
4. 1/2 cup ground almonds
5. rosewater according to your preference
6. 1/4 cup blanched slivered almonds
7. 1/4 cup white sugar

Directions:

1. Get some milk straight from the frig (two cups) and mix it with some corn starch.
2. Take the other cups of milk and combine it with the grounded almonds and cardamom. Once you have combined the cardamom and the almonds you want to mix this almond milk mix with the cornstarch milk and make sure to stir it all together nicely with a whisk.
3. At this point you may want to add more rose water or sugar according to your tastes.
4. Let everything boil for about three mins. Your level of heating should be medium.
5. Before serving the dish you want to take out the cardamom.
6. Add some additional almonds before serving as well.
7. Enjoy.

Serving Size: 6 servings

Preparation	Cooking	Total Time
≈ 15 mins		≈ 1 hr

Nutritional Information:

Calories	223 kcal
Carbohydrates	28.3 g
Cholesterol	7 mg
Fat	9.9 g
Fiber	1.9 g
Protein	6.2 g
Sodium	35 mg

* Percent Daily Values are based on a 2,000 calorie diet.

Sekanjabin

(Mint, Ginger, Strawberry Syrup)

Ingredients:

1. 4 cups white sugar
2. 2 cups water
3. 12 oz fresh or frozen strawberries, chopped
4. one cup chopped fresh mint
5. 1/2 cup sliced fresh ginger
6. 2 lemons, peeled and juiced
7. one cup white balsamic vinegar (not distilled vinegar)

Directions:

1. Get a nice sized saucepan that you can remove from the stove easily.
2. Add your sugar and water to this pot and get everything boiling with a high level of heat.
3. Continue to let the mixture boil until you find that sugar as dissolved.
4. Once you find that the sugar has dissolved you want to combine the following ingredients: lemon juice, strawberries, lemon peels, mint, and ginger.
5. Allow everything to continue cooking until you find that the mixture is bowling again. Once everything is boiling you want to lower the heating source to a medium level and let everything continue to simmer for 20 mins.

6. After 20 mins take the contents away from their heating source and mix in the white balsamic vinegar. You want the leave the mixture alone until it reaches a room temperature.
7. Once the contents have reached a room temperature, let it sit for about 8 hours or overnight.
8. After sitting overnight grab a good sieve and remove the fruit from the mixture. Keep the fruit in an airtight container at room temperature as well.
9. To serve use the following formula: 5 parts water to one part of syrup. Syrup should be served frigid.
10. Enjoy.

Serving Size: 6 cups of syrup

Adas Polow

(Rice and Lentils)

Ingredients:

1. one lb uncooked white rice
2. 4 cups water, or as needed
3. 1/2 tsp salt
4. 2 cups water, or more as needed
5. salt according to your preference
6. 2 cups dry lentils, rinsed
7. 1/4 cup vegetable oil, divided
8. 2 large onions, thinly sliced
9. 1/2 tsp saffron
10. 1/3 cup hot water
11. 3/4 cup pitted, chopped dates
12. 3/4 cup raisins

Directions:

1. To make this delicious recipe let's get a container to cover our rice in.
2. Put the rice in the container, possibly a bowl, and cover everything with water.
3. Allow the rice to sit covered for three hrs.
4. After three hrs remove the water from the rice.
5. Get a pan to cook the rice in.
6. Put about 4 cups of water and half of a tsp of salt in the pan with the rice and heat everything over a higher level of heating until you find that the water is boiling.

7. Once everything is boiling you want to lower the heating level to a lower to medium level of heat. Place a lid on the pan let it cook for about ten mins.
8. We only want our rice to get partially cooked, not fully cooked. After 10 mins of partial cooking take out the water from the rice.
9. Place the rice to the side to rest.
10. Grab another pan. Combine in the pan 2 cups of water with some salt.
11. Let the water and salt achieve a state of boiling. Once everything is boiling combine your lentils with the salted water.
12. Allow everything to begin boiling again. Once the lentils are boiling we want to lower the heating source down to a medium level.
13. Allow the lentils to continue simmering over the medium heat for about 20 mins. After 20 mins you want to take the lentils away from their heating source and let them rest.
14. Now you want to grab a medium to large sized frying pan or skillet and place in 2 tbsps of veggie oil.
15. Heat the oil over a medium level of heat to caramelize some onions.
16. Once your oil is hot add your onions and fry them for about 20 mins. Taking care to consistently stir them, so they do not burn. Once caramelized (cooked for 20 mins) place onions to the side for work later.
17. Grab your saffron and combine it with one third of a cup of water and place this to the side as well.

18. Now we want to grab another large pot that is deep and add to the pot, 2 tbsps of veggie oil. Once the oil is hot we want to remove half of the rice from earlier and cover the bottom of the pot with the rice.
19. Take your lentils and layer them over the rice. Now we want to grab the rest of the rice and place it over the lentils to make the final layer. In the end we should have rice at the bottom, lentils in the middle, and rice at the top.
20. Once you have created this layer you want to lower the heating source to its lowest level and place a lid on the pot, and allow everything to cook down until you find that the rice is nice and tender. This should take about 20 mins.
21. After the rice has been cooking for 20 mins you want to combine, with the rice, your saffron mixture, and allow everything to cook 10 more mins.
22. After 10 mins of cooking you should notice that the saffron has been fully integrated with the rice.
23. Take your rice and place it into a serving dish. Take care to cover the top of the rice with crusted harder rice from the bottom of the pan.
24. To garnish this dish you may want to add some fried onions or dates.
25. Enjoy

Serving Size: 8 servings

Preparation	Cooking	Total Time
20 mins	1 hr 15 mins	4 hrs 35 mins

Nutritional Information:

Calories	537 kcal
Carbohydrates	100.4 g
Cholesterol	0 mg
Fat	7.9 g
Fiber	17.7 g
Protein	17.7 g
Sodium	209 mg

* Percent Daily Values are based on a 2,000 calorie diet.

Lamb and Asparagus Stew

Ingredients:

1. 3 tbsps vegetable oil
2. one onion, chopped
3. 1/2 lb cubed lamb stew meat
4. 1/2 tsp salt
5. 1/2 tsp ground black pepper
6. one tbsp ground turmeric
7. 1/2 (6 oz) can tomato paste
8. one cup water
9. one clove garlic, chopped
10. one bunch fresh asparagus, trimmed and cut into one inch pieces

Directions:

1. To make this recipe grab a saucepan and add some veggie oil to it. You want to get this veggie oil nice and hot with a medium to higher level of heat before continuing.
2. Once you have your oil hot you want to combine your onions with it and fry everything for about two mins.
3. Combine the following with your onions: turmeric, lamb, pepper, and salt. You want to continue frying everything until you find that the lamb is fully cooked and has loss all of its pinkness on its outside.
4. The lamb should be cooked for about three mins with a higher level of heat. Take care to constantly stir the contents so nothing burns.

5. Combine with the lamb the following: garlic, tomato paste, and water. Allow everything to cook until you find that it is nicely simmering. Once you have gotten everything to simmer you want to lower the heat to a lower-to-medium level.
6. Place a lid over the lamb and let everything simmer for 25 mins. After 25 mins of simmering combine with the lamb, some asparagus, and let this cook for another three mins.
7. Plate and enjoy.

Serving Size: 2 servings

Preparation	Cooking	Total Time
20 mins	35 mins	55 mins

Nutritional Information:

Calories	503 kcal
Carbohydrates	30.5 g
Cholesterol	64 mg
Fat	33.5 g
Fiber	9.2 g
Protein	25.6 g
Sodium	980 mg

* Percent Daily Values are based on a 2,000 calorie diet.

Persian Yogurt Dessert

Ingredients:

1. 2 cups plain yogurt
2. 1/4 cup sour cream
3. one tbsp dried dill weed
4. one tbsp dried mint
5. 1/2 cucumber, peeled, seeded, and diced
6. 1/2 cup chopped walnuts
7. 1/2 cup raisins
8. 3 whole walnuts
9. 6 raisins for decorating

Directions:

1. So to begin we want to grab a container that is good for mixing, preferably a bowl.
2. Combine and mix the following ingredients with a whisk: mint, yogurt, dill, and sour cream. Take care to whisk everything evenly so you have a nice smooth mixture afterwards.
3. Combine the following ingredients with your mixture: half a cup of raisins, cucumber, and walnuts that have been chopped.
4. Mix everything together evenly.
5. Garnish this dish with more raisins and also some whole walnuts.
6. Enjoy.

Serving Size: 3 cups

Preparation	Cooking	Total Time

| 15 mins | | 15 mins |

Nutritional Information:

Calories	186 kcal
Carbohydrates	18.7 g
Cholesterol	9 mg
Fat	10.6 g
Fiber	1.4 g
Protein	6.9 g
Sodium	66 mg

* Percent Daily Values are based on a 2,000 calorie diet.

Jarjeer

(Arugula Salad)

Ingredients:

1. one bunch arugula
2. 2 onions, thinly sliced
3. one cup chopped mushrooms
4. one tomato, diced (optional)
5. one tsp extra virgin olive oil
6. 1/2 lemon, juiced
7. 2 tsps sumac (see Note)
8. Salt according to your preference

Directions:

1. Before we can use our leaves of arugula we have to wash them and let them dry.
2. Once your leaves have been washed fully. Put them on a big plate and cover them with tomato, mushrooms, and onions.
3. Now get a smaller sized mixing dish and combine the following: sumac, olive oil, and lemon juice.
4. Also add some salt to the mix according to your preference.
5. Combine all the seasonings with a whisk.
6. Enjoy

NOTE: The sumac spice is made from the berries of an interesting bushy plant that grows in the

Mediterranean. Check your local Arab or Indian store for this spice. It has a very strong but good taste.

Serving Size: 4 servings

Preparation	Cooking	Total Time
15 mins		15 mins

Nutritional Information:

Calories	62 kcal
Carbohydrates	10.4 g
Cholesterol	0 mg
Fat	1.8 g
Fiber	2.9 g
Protein	3.2 g
Sodium	119 mg

* Percent Daily Values are based on a 2,000 calorie diet.

Persian Melon Salad

Ingredients:

1. one honeydew melon, fruit removed with a melon baller
2. one cantaloupe, fruit removed with a melon baller
3. 1/4 watermelon, fruit removed with a melon baller
4. one bunch grapes
5. one pineapple - peeled, cored, and cut into chunks
6. 2 tbsps pickled ginger
7. one cup fresh orange juice
8. 1/4 cup fresh lime juice
9. one tbsp white sugar
10. 1/4 cup chopped fresh mint
11. one pint fresh strawberries, hulled (optional)
12. 4 sprigs fresh mint for garnish

Directions:

1. Grab a good container for mixing, possibly a bowl, and combine the following ingredients: mint that has been chopped, honeydew, sugar, watermelon, lime juice, grapes, orange juice, pineapple, and pickled ginger.
2. Take care to mix the ingredients nicely.
3. After mixing your fruit, place a covering on the container, and put it in the frig for about one hour. The longer the better.

4. Before serving add your strawberries and also some mint.
5. Enjoy.

Serving Size: 12 servings

Preparation	Cooking	Total Time
30 mins		1 hr 30 mins

Nutritional Information:

Calories	194 kcal
Carbohydrates	48.8 g
Cholesterol	0 mg
Fat	0.9 g
Fiber	4.3 g
Protein	2.8 g
Sodium	47 mg

* Percent Daily Values are based on a 2,000 calorie diet.

A Gift From Me To You...

I know you like cultural food. But what about Japanese Sushi?

Join my private mailing list of readers and get a copy of *Infinite Sushi: A Complete Set of Sushi and Japanese Recipes* by fellow BookSumo author Hashimoto Kazuma for FREE!

http://booksumo.com/a-kitchen-in-persia-classical-persian-recipes/

Enjoy some of the best sushi available!

You will also receive updates about all my new books when they are free. So please show your support.

Also don't forget to like and subscribe on the social networks. I love meeting my readers. Links to all my profiles are below so please click and connect :)

Facebook

Twitter

Google +

Come On...
Let's Be Friends :)

I adore my readers and love connecting with them socially. Please follow the links below so we can connect on Facebook, Twitter, and Google+.

Facebook

Twitter

Google +

I also have a blog that I regularly update for my readers so check it out below.

My Blog

ABOUT THE PUBLISHER.

BookSumo specializes in providing the best books on special topics that you care about. *A Kitchen In Persia: Classical and Unique Persian Recipes* will take you on a trip to Iran with simple and delicious recipes.

To find out more about BookSumo and find other books we have written go to:

http://booksumo.com/.

CAN I ASK A FAVOUR?

If you found this book interesting, or have otherwise found any benefit in it. Then may I ask that you post a review of it on Amazon? Nothing excites me more than new reviews, especially reviews which suggest new topics for writing. I do read all reviews and I always factor feedback into my newer works.

So if you are willing to take ten minutes to write what you sincerely thought about this book then please visit our Amazon page and post your opinions.

Again thank you!

Interested in My Other Cookbooks?

Check out some of my similar cookbooks on different cultural food like:

Egypt, Morocco, Persia, & Pakistan:

Arabia & Asia: A Cookbook with Recipes from Egypt, Morocco, Persia, & Pakistan

Lebanon:

Classical Lebanese Cooking: Simple, Easy, and Unique Lebanese Recipes

India:

Classical Indian Cooking: Simple, Easy, and Unique Indian Recipes

Printed in Great Britain
by Amazon